"*Spiritual Inspirations*"

*A collection of poems birthed out of trials
and tribulations; a personal testimony to
encourage and bring inner healing to
others.*

Written by

Prophetess Valerie A. Brown

Table of Contents

Part 1

Praise and Worship   pg. 1

The Poetry Within...3

When I Awoke This Morning..............................4

My Best Friend...6

The Love Of My Life 7

Totally Committed 8

Thank You 9

Part 2

Encouragement I   pg.11

Success In Christ 13

Prayer Changes Things...................................15

Refocused 16

Come To Jesus Just As You Are 18

Rest In Me...19

Part 3

Pain & Suffering I   pg. 21

I Thought Life Was Over 23

Strengthen Me...25

Lord, Sweet Lord 26

Blown Away 27

Please Forgive Me..29

After All This 30

Table of Contents

Part 4

Spiritual Warfare   **pg. 33**

Spirit Of Hatred 35

Beware Of Satan 37

Spirit Of Fear 38

Highway To Hell 40

I Can't Understand 42

To Hell From The Church 43

Part 5

Pain and Suffering II   **pg.45**

Love Yourself No Matter What 47

A Wounded Child 49

Chances 50

Paying The Price 52

I'm Not Special 54

Reasons 56

The Love For My Unborn Child 58

Part 6

Encouragement II   **pg. 61**

It's Time To Go Back 63

Let Your Light Shine 65

Be An Overcomer 66

Feed My Sheep 70

Until We Meet Again 71

Part 1
Praise and Worship

The Poetry Within

The poetry within flows and flows like a river,
one of many waters. A flow that is never
ending; there to transition on a mission to
quench every thirst.

The poetry within flows and flows like music;
a sweet melody to heal all bruises. A
medicine to mend and heal the broken heart;
transcending the mind and the soul.
Releasing the fears, comforting each and
every tear.

The gift of God, poetry within flows and flows
like a river, one of many waters. A flow that
is never ending, there to transition on a
mission to quench every thirst.

When I Awoke This Morning

Oh, how happy I was just to see another day;
when I awoke this morning! Life, health and
strength, activities of my limbs. A right and
sane mind in the midst of disastrous times.
I heard the birds sing, the joy bells ring and
the airplanes flying by. I was thankful for
hearing when I awoke this morning! Cool,
crisp breeze blowing through the air. Rain
showers, the touch of God's hand, His breath
blown upon man.

The aroma of flowers blooming in the air, oh
how thankful I was to be able to smell! No
blessing is ever too small to tell. Oh, how
happy I was just to be able to smell! When I
awoke this morning; I was able to see God's
beauty in his creation.

How miraculous, dazzling and fabulous! Able
to move about, raising my hands in a dance
as I give a shout. On this glorious morning
some didn't make it, we must be grateful.
Oh, taste and see that the Lord is good. Oh,

how happy I was just to see another day

when I awoke this morning!

My Best Friend

He is a ten, the only friend I ever had able to
stay in my life situations and circumstances,
from beginning to end. Through the trials,
tribulations, persecutions, self-destruction
too; Christ was there pushing me to make it
through.
Forsaken by many doesn't matter anymore,
for he taught me real love comes only from
above. Now I'm free to know the difference
and accept my weakness and pray for the
ignorant.

Free to celebrate, dance and leap. Free from
abuse, torment and pain; going through life
keeping me sane. He alone has the power to
do what he has done. Giving me the strength
to take a licking and keep on ticking.

Forgiving me when I am wrong, in my
sorrowful heart, giving me a song. He is a
ten, my best friend. The only friend I ever
had able to stay in my life situations and
circumstances from beginning to end.

The Love Of My Life

The love of my life brings pleasure, success
and completeness to my life. Redemption,
justification, you love me with demonstration;
grace and mercy you bestow upon me. Your
favor brings about blessing after blessing,
able to release doubt, fear, all stressing.

A love that's pure, true and sure. The love of
my life makes everything alright. Storms,
trials seem trivial in his sight. No other love
could compare, he is so awesome; his love he
shares. With open arms stretched ooh so
wide, his love awaits to dwell inside.

A love that heals, secures and saves you too,
the only love of his kind, I dare you to try.
Come see, taste his love, ever so great. You
will never be the same; the love of my life he
will change your name. The love of my life
brings pleasure, success, and completeness
to my life.

Totally Committed

Totally committed not about to quit it, I must commit to your will and to your way. Here not just for a season, but here to stay, never needing a reason. Your love I've never known, freely given to call my own.

Totally committed to the word of God; meditating, allowing it to live inside. The joy you give is an ultimate pleasure, unable to compare to any earthly treasure. The peace of God that guards, protects, renews the mind.

Totally committed not about to quit it. I must commit to your will and your way. Here not just for a season, but here to stay, never needing a reason.

Thank You

Saying thank you doesn't merely seem enough for the one I love, honor, respect so much. Thanking you for life, health and strength. For salvation, the cost is free; how is that possible or able to be?

Thanking you for the miracles that come my way, day after day. So grateful that you alone have the very last say. Thanking you for my goals and dreams, giving me possibility, believing in me, giving me responsibility.

For choosing me, appointing me, anointing me too, saying thank you doesn't merely seem enough, for the one I love, honor, respect so much. Thank you for the Holy Spirit that comforts me, who resides in me.

Thanking you for the call upon my life, spiritual insight. For loving me; being family, a true friend, staying by my side till the very end. Thank you for the good, the bad, ups and downs, for delivering me, embracing me, resurrecting me. Most of all thanks for saving me! Saying thank you doesn't merely seem enough for the one I love, honor, respect so much.

Part 2

Encouragement I

Success In Christ

Completely surrendering to Christ is when success will take over your life. Submit and cast all your cares on him. Making you complete, he will be whatever you need him to be.

That job or career, placed in the front, no longer the rear. All things are possible with Christ in your life. Greater is he that is in me than he that is in the world. Family and friends to know salvation through your prayers.

With amazing grace, a chosen spouse, possibilities are endless; with Christ in your life. Beautiful children when the doctor said it would never be. Christ steps in and allows it to be.

The past is gone, receive a new start; receive your rewards and desires of your heart, for this is the word. Achieving through Christ, he will see you through. Success can be yours, you must tell the story.

To all men and women, both boy and girl, reach for the top and achieve your goals, give your life and prepare yourself to receive success in Christ. Completely surrendering to Christ is when success will take over your life.

Prayer changes things; removing the difficulties of every situation, giving you a song to sing. It changes, rearranges circumstances, situations, frustrations, sickness and diseases. Christ came to heal and set the captive free.

Put your trust in God, you must believe. Pray, holler, scream, the master came to redeem. Cast down, pull down every strong hold and evil report with the words of your mouth, through prayer there's power, release all that doubt.

If only you would believe, you would receive. He caused the blind to see, the lame to walk, the deaf to hear; go ahead cast aside those fears. Prayer changes things; removing the difficulties of ever situation, giving you a song to sing.

Refocused, refocused, focused I am, escaping by the blood, the enemies plan. Endangered mind, finally free to rid the evil and gain the good. Open to receive what I need, releasing negativity that dwelled within me.

Handicapped no longer crippled by life. I'm refocused and stronger than ever; able to stand, no need to fall. Focused I am, no longer a slave of abuse or tolerating any misuse.

Goodbye old sinful life; your misery, pain and strife. I am free to live a refocused life; a life of success and joy, God's peace straight from heavens throne! My life has changed, refocused I am, rearranged.

Anointed my eyes for me to see, no more fog, spiritual glaucoma or disease. Obedience came once refocused. Oh, what joy to live accordingly. Anointed my ears for me to hear, no more tingling in my ear, all is crystal

clear. Refocused, refocused, focused I am,
escaping by the blood, the enemies plan.

Come To Jesus Just As You Are

Come to Jesus just as you are, he never
promised you tomorrow. Trying to wait,
thinking you can get it right, all have come
short and sinned in his sight.

Come to Jesus just as you are; alcohol,
prostitute and drugs, don't go through life,
crippled with a limp. Liar, thief, fornicator,
adulterer too, don't be fooled.

Lust of money, hypocrite, backslider,
outraged, he loves us all the same. It's the
sin he hates, he died on the cross and
salvation came.

Come to Jesus just as you are, changing
your possibilities into realities. Come to
Jesus just as you are, he never promised you
tomorrow.

Rest In Me

Rest in me I say; don't worry, doubt or fear,
but go ahead and rest in me. Allow your soul
to heal and mend, for I will set you free!

I will bless you and exalt you too, all in due
time, for these are promises of mine. For I
love you with an everlasting love. Prepare
yourself to receive from above, keep your eyes
on me and I will give you peace.

For I am in control and I will make you
whole. Rest in me I say; don't worry, doubt,
or fear, but go ahead and rest in me. I'll stick
closer than any brother. I'll carry you all the
way and take you further.

Your comforter and deliverer for you to see
cast your cares all upon me. In the midst of
the trial, I will restore; turn your frown into a
smile. Rest in me I say; don't worry, doubt or
fear, but go ahead and rest in me.

Part 3
Pain & Suffering I

I Thought Life Was Over

I thought life was over, but God said not so.
A new beginning, ending sorrow, hope for
tomorrow.

Rejection, so I was stressing. Unloved so I
was ruff. Misunderstood so I believed no
good. Mistreated so I lived defeated. Raped
so I would take, then push love away.

Delayed and denied, wanting to die. I
thought life was over, but God said not so...
My life seemed over, and so many times I
couldn't understand why I was still alive.

Now, I understand he had a plan; In spite of
it all. Now I am a witness and I will stand tall.
I thought life was over, But God said not so.

Believe in me; for you are my daughter for the
world to see. Rejection and now I'm
affectionate, unloved, I'm kind, tender as a
dove. Misunderstood, I stand boldly
proclaiming Christ as I should

Raped; I give love, I embrace love. No longer
do I push love away. Delayed and denied, yet
I'm determined to live and not die. I thought
life was over, but God said not so, a new
beginning, ending sorrow, hope for tomorrow.

Strengthen Me

When I am weak and can't see, I ask you Lord to strengthen me. Let your anointing fall fresh upon my soul, in my youth and when I am old.

Give me the strength to do what is right, not falling into the deepness of the night. Set a guard at my mouth that I may watch what I say, strengthen me to endure every day.

With your power and might, I will win each and every fight. Enable me to stand, give me your sight. Flesh and Satan dare to be strong; your strength Lord will keep me from doing wrong.

In my weakness and times of storms, I'll look up to heaven and remember you're never far. When I am weak and cannot see, I ask you Lord to strengthen me.

Lord, Sweet Lord

Lord, sweet Lord! I wonder how and why.
Why some say they love you, slipping and
sliding, constantly backsliding.

Never smiling nor having a kind word;
playing judge, jury and prosecutor in the
church on duty!!! Praising your name all day,
up in the church, I'll proclaim your name.

Reminiscing, shaking hands, Praise God; as
we say good-bye it happens once more trying
to reach for the door.

Fiery darts; words that cut, exchanged in the
house, leaving me hurt, bleeding with rage
and doubt. But Lord, sweet Lord I remember
you and all you went through!

The hanging, humiliation and horrific
beating. Through it all you were never
defeated. Not again and never to be, will I
allow one to hinder me. Keep me; hide me in
your word Lord, sweet Lord!

Blown Away

Tossed and driven blown away while trying to
learn the biblical way. Not yet rooted or
grounded, religious folks looking down upon
me frowning.

First it was my dress, with nothing else to
wear! Blown away by the arrogant stares.
Then it was my hair not quite the right style.

Make-up, jewelry, accessories too, never able
to please the religious crew. Then it was my
shoes and the tension grew. Desperately
trying time after time, hiding the grief that
was deep inside.

Blown away you see, how could church be for
me, the more I tried the more criticized.
Protocol, rules, regulations, so unsure, yet I
here Christ saying I must endure.

I hear their words and see the beam in their
eyes; I will deliver if you continue to try.
Come to me just as you are. I will deliver
when times get hard. Tossed and driven,

blown away, while trying to learn the biblical way.

I'm asking for your forgiveness when I was
wicked and bitter. Crucified you over and
over and I apologize. Today I'm saved,
changed and sanctified.

Because of your grace I'm free today. I'm
asking for your forgiveness when I was
wicked and bitter. Time after time, I let you
down. Blessed by you, still wearing a frown.

Because of your goodness, I walk in
forgiveness. I'm asking for your forgiveness
when I was wicked and bitter. Walking in
fear and doubt with endless tears.

Because of your mercy I'm alive to try; free to
receive, changed and saved with heaven
promised as my home. I'm asking for your
forgiveness when I was wicked and bitter.

After All This

After all this, I am as strong as the wind! Getting through life's worst still bearing a grin. After all the pain, thunderstorms, pouring down rain, I'm able to shine bright as a star. To believe in my dreams whether near or far.

To find myself again was a personal goal. After all this I realize what doesn't kill you makes' you stronger; greater than ever!

Though it seemed this time in life that I was travelling through a tunnel with very little light. A very long journey, but I finally made it out. Standing here at the end of this tunnel I see a light; a light that's shining ever so bright.

Overwhelmed with joy I began to cry yet chose to dry my eyes. Finally, I found myself again, oh the joy and peace within. Sometimes there are questions of how and why, but I hear the voice of my savior saying never mind.

Live for today, dream of tomorrow, believe in
yourself, praise God, for he is the answer
after all this.

Part 4
Spiritual Warfare

Spirit Of Hatred

Spirit of hatred, spirit of hatred, not attempting to hide, standing there cruel and blatant! That mean and nasty spirit, still on the rise. So be careful, keep watch and not let it rise.

Hear it in the voice; see it in the eyes of those who choose the enemy every time. To be used by the enemy at any given time, causing dis-order, division, and chaos all the time.

Rebellion, disobedience is on the rise, so be careful, keep watch; don't let it rise. Anger, resentment, bitterness too, throwing tantrums, manipulating you. A smile in your face, with a look of disgrace. A stab in your back with a wicked jab.

Cut so deep only God could heal, expose, reveal. The plan, the plot, the scheme of man, hidden behind the enemy's plan.

Spirit of hatred, spirit of hatred, not attempting to hide standing there cruel and blatant. That mean and nasty spirit still on the rise. So be careful, keep watch and not let it rise.

Beware Of Satan

Beware of Satan for he doesn't play fair! Like a lion he will roar to chase you scared. Beware of Satan who fights till the end.

When you think he's gone, he's back again; to cause confusion, grief and pain. Satan comes to bring you shame. He attempts to take you out; he's not playing a game. Plead the blood, rebuke Satan in Jesus name.

He may not fall right away, continue to plead the blood, he will be destroyed anyway. He'll hang on as long as he can, you must be strong and rebuke him anyway. Beware of Satan for he doesn't play fair, like a lion he will roar to chase you scared!

Spirit Of Fear

Spirit of fear, spirit of fear, why have you
come to sit and draw so near? What does
God have for me that you won't let me be?
What breakthrough is near that you must
stop and stare?

You have come to paralyze, strip me and
terrorize me. Unable to think clear, confused
and hindered when gripped by fear.
Listening to your shouts you send out, all full
of nothing but doubt. All up in my ear, I will
conquer you fear.

Spirit of fear, spirit of fear, why have you
come to sit and draw so near? Your voice
may be loud, but God's voice is louder, and
no other voice will I follow!

So, go ahead and do what you must; but
because of God's love, I will continue to trust.
See, you are just the stepping stone to what
God has for me; so, it doesn't matter go
ahead and continue to tease. I'll conquer you
once again; see you were never my friend.

I can do all things through Christ Jesus who strengthens me, and I know you know the word, so now let me set you free! Remember the word Satan and what it says,

God has not come to give me "you" spirit of fear, so I rebuke you now, you can't sit here.

You know that God came to give me love, straight from above. He came to give me power, so you must leave not tomorrow, but this very same hour.

A sound mind that's what he said, so take your confusion and not another tear will I shed. Spirit of fear, spirit of fear you've got to move, I tell you now I am through.

Highway To Hell

On the highway to hell doing 70mph not looking nor caring with Satan as the driver. Leading you, guiding you in all your ways on the highway to hell heading for your grave.

To destroy you is his plan and here all along, you were his greatest fan. Playing you for a fool, carrying you around like you were his tool. On the highway to hell, cheating, stealing, gang-banging, drug-dealing for the heck of it, out there killing.

Drinking every day is another game; alcohol has become your middle name. Sex an object and now you have aides on the highway to hell wondering who to blame.

Satan will not be fulfilled until you are dead, buried and burning in hell. Bring your burdens all to Christ, he will help you, give you strength and might.

Don't you want a mind that's' sound, come
on, and get off that merry go round. Come
on, get off that highway to hell doing 70mph,
not looking or caring with Satan as the
driver.

I Can't Understand

I can't understand how you hear of my savior and still not believe; to disgrace his name with no fear or shame, to harden your heart and change his word; add to the word, chose and decide what you want from the word.

Rebellion, disbelief in a world of sin with no relief, except you know Christ Jesus. Blasphemy, witch-craft, works of flesh, sin at large at its best. It really doesn't matter you see, God will be God no matter what you believe.

The sun will still shine, the air remains for you to breathe, until the day comes for you to leave. Will you believe then, in the end? Will you still have a chance in the end? I can't understand how you hear of my savior and still not believe.

To Hell From The Church

Don't go to hell from the church, with Christ waiting to quench your ever-longing thirst. Tell me how much sense does' that make to sit week after week in the services of God; learn the word of God and be baptized.

Why speak in tongues, dance, sing and praise God, and then walk out the door only to deny. You deny him through your actions, your words and unchanged heart. The way you treat another, assisting your sister, while dogging your brother.

The homeless and hungry are invisible to you, be ever so careful, one day this could be you. Never a witness, nor speaking of salvation, but quick to curse and call damnation. Don't go to hell from the church, with Christ to quench your ever-longing thirst.

Part 5
Pain and Suffering II

Love Yourself No Matter What

Arise, stand and strut, love yourself no matter what. Why love everyone else, except yourself, love yourself no matter what.

Listening to the enemy and what he has to say, living your live in a destructive way. Low self-esteem with God-given dreams; depressed and stressed.

Don't be deceived by what you see, keep your eyes focused on Christ with purpose. You can get through it, if you allow it, love yourself no matter what.

When you are weak, he is strong, you must have faith, keep holding on. Your change will come if your heart is right, repent be cleansed from the sin within.

When you least expect it, your change will come; be ready at all times to receive from above. Trials come to make you strong, going through doesn't mean that you were wrong.

Crying is not weakness, its humility, strength and meekness. Christ came to heal your brokenness, wounds and sickness. All power is in this hand, only trust, believe; obey his commands.

Arise, stand and strut, love yourself no matter what. Why love everyone else except yourself, love yourself no matter what.

A Wounded Child

A wounded child, timid and shy; afraid to
open up, since life's been so ruff. A child
inside yet grown and mature on the outside.
Carrying the wounds year after year; stuck in
a standstill living in fear.

Rejected, wounded, and misunderstood,
early on in life's childhood. Rescued from
disaster through Christ who became my
master. Savior and friend till the very end.

Rescued from destruction, he taught me how
to function. With an inner voice, the Holy
Spirit became my source. Filling my heart
with his love, opening up, he taught me to
trust.

Healing me and giving me peace. Joy and
laughter, he continued rescuing me from
disaster. Arise I say, arise my wounded
child, timid and shy.

Chances

Chances, chances, romancing God, he gives
us chance after chance to get it right inside.
Tomorrow is not promised, get it right today.
God covers and protects those who obey.

Grace and mercy released for us, sin and evil
he frowns upon. Our God is a God of love, he
forgives and cleanses, but he is also judge. A
God of wrath, who warns us of our sin, gives
us chance after chance to repent of our sin

Again and again should we continue to sin.
God forbid, did you read your bible about the
consuming fire? "He loves me anyway," we
say, be warned not to live life just any kind of
way.

Woe unto you like Sodom and Gomorrah, he
loves us all, it's the sin he hates, don't be
fooled by repeating the same mistakes. We
shall be judged for every action, repent get it
right, today, don't wait till tomorrow.

Crystal clear is the word of God, woe unto
you who attempts to change the word.
Chances, chances, romancing God, he gives
us chance after chance to get it right inside...

Paying The Price

Why does it always seem like I'm the only one paying a price for everything in life having to sacrifice?

Doing without the things I love most, hard-pressed, heartaches, no need to boast. Why does it always seem like I'm the only one paying a price for everything in life, having to sacrifice.

Watching folks laid back; still getting by, not a care in the world wanting nothing out of life. Plotting and scheming, there life has no meaning.

Unwilling to change; living life in the fast lane. A trick of the enemy causing me to believe the thoughts of Satan, I won't be deceived. We all go through in life, having to pay a price.

Though the cost may not be the same it is what it is with no one to blame. So, I will pay the price as a living sacrifice.

For Christ we know paid the ultimate price.
Pay the price whatever the cost, don't be
deceived, fooled and lost

For once and for all; I need to accept, believe
that I am special. Stop tripping on God,
being selfish. Downplaying who I really am,
worried about others, but it's time for me to
believe, time to be free.

The apple of his eye is who he says that I
am, to accept the truth is his master plan.
Doubt has to leave and faith must be. The
word of God must be my reality.

Why am I saying that I am a nobody with
God's spirit inside? I must be somebody!
Why am I saying I can't be the best, when
God says I can pass each and every test?

Why am I saying my dreams can't come true;
when God says all things are possible?
Negativity and the attack on the mind, comes
from Satan to destroy you over time.

Cast it down with the word of God, he came
to give you life. For once and for all you need

to accept, believe that you are special. Stop
tripping on God, being selfish.

Reasons

A little bit of this! A little bit of that! Reasons, reasons, so many reasons why we abort a life a baby inside. In the eyes of a God who created mankind but see we don't have the right to take away a life.

With no one to blame but the enemy of God; Satan's in and out of the human mind. Cast down his thoughts and his opinions too, if not your very life he will take from you.

From the time you conceived; a miracle of life, a baby inside, thriving to survive, growing day by day, by Gods' amazing grace.

Created unique for the world to see, Like Dr. Martin King; let Freedom ring. Created with a dream and purpose from above. From our savior and king, let freedom ring. We don't have the right to take away a life.

I always wondered in my mind, how we take away a life, then say that it is right...from the

beginning of time, God knew you all the time.
In the womb of your mother, you were knit
together to live with him forever.

Your frame was not hidden in the secret
place. The birth of life an act of grace, from
the God of heaven who wove you together.

Your unformed body he knew you all the
time. Predestined life created just for you.
Fashioned in his image, blew breathe in you.
What an awesome father who created
mankind.

The author of life who created time. See we
don't have the right to take away a life. A
little bit of this! A little bit of that! Reasons,
reason, so many reasons why we abort a life
a baby inside, in the eyes of a God who
created mankind but see we don't have the
right to take away a life.

The Love For My Unborn Child

A cry from inside from a mother who lost a
child, the unborn child she carried inside.
Nightmares, heartaches, screams of sorrow
no hope for tomorrow.

Darkness, oppression, agony, a prisoner for
life never to be free. A sample, brief example
of the grief, burden, and pain I feel as I try to
comprehend why I lost my child, gave up my
child, my unborn child I carried inside.

Undeserving of the death you encountered;
deserved life, love and laughter. Abortion,
adoption, so finalized, no forgiveness of
yourself.

Issues, poverty, rape, pushing you into the
ultimate mistake. Molested, deserted, left
alone to fend for your own; still pushing you.

Threatened, bullied, and overwhelming fear;
pushing you into your greatest nightmare.

The Love For My Unborn Child

(continued)

Many hurdles, cross-roads, struggles and
problems.

Abortion is not the answer let God help you
through. You can make it! In times of
despair pray to God; find a friend, a Christian
who cares.

If you been here it's okay forgive yourself, let
God heal you today. A second chance he will
give you. Open up let God heal you...a cry
from inside, from a mother who lost the
unborn child she carried inside.

Part 6
Encouragement II

It's Time To Go Back

It's time, it's time; I watched you, my child,
endure the pain and then backslide. I long
for you, come back to me to be whole and
declare the victory.

Through all the hurt and strife, I still have a
plan for your life. Destruction and disaster,
it was me carrying you, Christ your master.

Wanting to die, I embraced you. Shielded
you, protected you, still I took the blame from
you. There for you all the time, but you
refuse to listen, I watched you walk away and
backslide.

I long for you, come back to me to be whole
and declare the victory. Journey after
journey still you made it out, mind crowded
with misery and doubt.

Journey after journey; I pulled you out,
though you couldn't see the end, a victory
shout! I kissed you, loved you, was there for

you night and day, still you decided to walk
away.

Longing for the day of your return; to come
running quickly into my arms. To father and
nurture you; to strengthen and heal your

Broken heart to fulfill my promise of a brand
new start.

Its time, it's time, I watched you my child,
endure the pain and then backslide. I long
for you, come back to me, to be whole and
declare the victory.

Let Your Light Shine

Let your light shine for the world to see, they must see Christ in you and in me. In your demeanor, in your talk, be an example in your everyday walk.

Let your light shine in such away, to brighten another's day. For the world to see a love so strong, knowing exactly where to go, when things go wrong.

In times of trials, tribulations and rumors of war; through your light the world will receive joy. Peace within getting through life's worst yet bearing a grin.

Let your light shine for many don't know the power of God or the excellence of his name. Let your light shine for the world to see, let them see Christ in you and in me.

Be An Overcomer

Stand there anyhow and be an overcomer!
God needs people that are stronger than ever.
Resisting Satan who is always attempting to
be clever.

Strong enough to know that God will deliver.
He alone will bring you into the place called
destiny. Don't give up when times get hard;
set-backs, disappointments, persecution too,
stand there anyhow and be an overcomer.

When it seems as though there is nothing
else that you can do, and all you see is
difficult situations facing you; be still and
know the master will carry you.

Go ahead and release all those fears.
Release the hurt, pain and tears. Don't wait
till the battles over shout now, you have been
set free no longer bound. Hallelujah, a
reason to praise and worship our holy God.

For we have been washed, changed, restored
inside. Be strong like the wind for your able

to do all things through Christ who
strengthens you.

Look past the devices, contrary spirits, faces
of people not yet delivered. You must stand

There anyhow and overcome! God needs
people that are stronger than ever.

After You Suffered Awhile

After you suffered awhile you shall be
established. That's what I heard him say, so
rest assure, there will be a new day.

Job lost everything he had, even his children
those who called him dad. He suffered for
quite a while, felt alone and placed on trial.
After the suffering, he received double for all
his troubles.

Set up by God yet established after a while.
Joseph was called, chosen, appointed by
God; still he suffered for quite a while.

Sold into slavery by his very own brothers,
jealous for their father loved him more than
the others. From the pit to the palace, then
the prison you see, everywhere he went, he
was placed in authority.

What God has for you is for you, but we
must go through. Troubles don't last always
and you shall be established.

After you suffered awhile, you shall be
established, that's what I heard him say, so
rest assure, there will be a new day

Feed My Sheep

If you love me feed my sheep; don't allow
them to be fragile and weak. Feed them the
word to know my power, to know there is
strength when they are tired.

Feed them the word to know my promises
that they shall reap and receive in time. Feed
them the word to know salvation,
sanctification and deliverance.

Give them the word to bring light,
edification, creativity in a cold, dark and evil
world. If you love me, feed my sheep; don't
allow them to be fragile and weak.

Until We Meet Again

Until we meet again, I'll continue to pray for you my friend. The gift of poetry to bring encouragement; lighten your heart with a brand new start. Truth, enrichment and healing all in the name of Jesus I pray.

Until we meet again, I'll continue to pray for you my friend. Don't give up when times get hard, continue to pray, and you will go far.

Listen to the voice of Christ, he will be your strength, give power and might. Stand alone if you must, but I pray you remain strong and refuse to do wrong.

Nothing in life is worth giving up this fight, he is worth it all, and we must learn to stand tall. May his peace be with you, until we meet again. Until we meet again, I'll continue to pray for you my friend.

About the Author

Valerie is a gifted writer, dancer, and poet. She has walked in these gifts since an early age. Her writings consist of poetry, songs, skits, and plays. Valerie also conducts workshops for pre-publishing, Bullying & Suicide, Depression, Singles and Dance Ministry. Valerie was licensed as an Evangelist in 1995 and in 1998 she was called into the office of Prophetess and attended "The School of Prophets." Valerie was ordained as an Elder in 2004. She also attended and graduated from "The Black Ministries Program" at Hartford Seminary. In 2016 Valerie also established "Diamonds, Rubies & Pearls", a women's outreach ministry which includes a weekly conference call prayer line, monthly fellowships and an annual healing retreat.

Other Books Available

1. Spiritual Inspirations
2. Family Affairs
3. Matters of the Heart
4. Champions
5. In My Time of Grief
6. A Stand Against Youth Bullying And Suicide*

* Also available on DVD – A Stand Against Youth Bullying And Suicide

Contact

For more information, contact

Valerie A. Brown

email @

Royaltybydivine@gmail.com

Or

via phone @

(203) 514-0186

Made in the USA
Columbia, SC
30 January 2021